UPDATED EDITION

Guess What!

Student's Book **3B**

with eBook

American English

Susannah Reed with Kay Bentley

Series Editor: Lesley Koustaff

CAMBRIDGE

Contents

Home time

Look!

Guess What!

1 🎧 5.01 **Listen and point.**

2 🎧 5.02 **Listen, point, and repeat.**

3 🎧 5.03 **Listen and answer the questions.**

1. Is he drinking juice? Yes, he is.

4 Think **Describe and guess the numbers.**

She's making a cake. Number 9!

1 drink juice
2 eat a sandwich
3 do the dishes
4 play on the computer
5 read a book
6 watch TV
7 do homework
8 listen to music
9 make a cake
10 wash the car

5 🎧 5.04 Sing the song.

We are all different,
In my family.
We are all different,
My family and me.

I like listening to music,
But I don't like reading books.
My mom loves reading books,
But she doesn't like watching TV.

My sister enjoys watching TV,
But she doesn't like making cakes.
My dad loves making cakes,
But he doesn't like listening to music.

6 Make sentences about the song and say who.

He enjoys listening to music.   Alex!

7 (About Me) Ask and answer with your friend. Then tell another friend.

Do you like playing on the computer?

Yes, I do. I love playing on the computer.

Ellie loves playing on the computer.

Remember!

He **likes** liste**ning** to music.
He **doesn't like** read**ing** books.
She **enjoys** watch**ing** TV.
She **loves** play**ing** on the computer.

Grammar fun!

8 🎧 5.05 **Look at the photographs and choose. Then listen and repeat.**

1

Does he like playing on the computer?
Yes, he does. / No, he doesn't.

2

Does she enjoy washing the car?
Yes, she does. / No, she doesn't.

9 🎧 5.06 **Listen and find. Then answer the question.**

Pedro

Vivian

Fred

Lina

Anil

Camilla

10 **Ask and answer with a friend.**

Does Lina like doing homework?

Yes, she does.

11 🎧 5.07 **Go to page 102. Listen and repeat the chant.**

Remember!
Does he enjoy doing the dishes?
Yes, he does.   No, he doesn't.

Grammar fun!

Grammar

→ Workbook page 50

Skills: *Listening and speaking*

 Are you helpful at home?

12 **Listen and choose.**

1 Isabella likes / doesn't like cleaning her bedroom.
2 She enjoys / doesn't enjoy washing the car.
3 She likes / doesn't like doing the dishes.
4 Brad likes / doesn't like cleaning his bedroom.
5 He enjoys / doesn't enjoy washing his bike.
6 He enjoys / doesn't enjoy making cakes.

13 **Ask and answer with a friend.**

Do you like cleaning your bedroom?
Do you like washing the car?
Do you like doing the dishes?
Do you like making cakes?

Writing

➜ Workbook page 51: Write about being helpful at home.

1 Find a chocolate cake.

2 Let's make the cake.

My aunt Pat likes making cakes.

Great! Let's go to her house!

3 What do we need?

Eggs, milk, chocolate …

OK. Here we are.

4 This is fun!

Oh, dear! Anna loves chocolate cake!

Anna! Stop that!

5 Look! It's great!

Good job!

Let's add some chocolate eggs.

6 Let's put it in the …

Watch out, Lucas!

Oh, no!

7 Oh, dear! I'm so sorry.

Me, too!

Come on. Let's make another cake.

64 Value: Show forgiveness

→ Workbook page 52

15   **Listen and repeat. Then act.**

chocolate cake   cheese sandwich   carrot cake
sausage sandwich   chicken sandwich

1

Let's make a carrot cake.

What do we need?

Eggs, milk, carrots …

OK. Here we are.

2

Let's make a chicken sandwich.

What do we need?

Bread, chicken …

Say it!

16 **Listen and repeat.**

Panthers learn to hunt three months after birth.

panthers

→ Workbook page 53   Function: Suggesting food to make   Pronunciation: *th* **65**

Where do
people
live?

1 🎧 5.12 Listen and repeat.

1 countryside

2 village

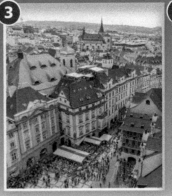
3 town

4 city

2 CLIL ▶ Watch the video.

3 What can you see in the pictures?

1

2

3

4

Guess What!
There are more chickens in the world than people.

Let's collaborate!

OUR **HELPING HANDS** SCHEDULE

M T W T F S

agree
plan
compare
people
help
create

4 Where would you like to live?

6 Hobbies

Look!

Guess What!

1 🎧 6.01 **Listen and point.**

2 🎧 6.02 **Listen, point, and repeat.**

Weekend Clubs and Activities

music clubs

craft clubs

sports clubs

3 🎧 6.03 **Listen and say the numbers.**

4 Think **Ask questions and guess the numbers.**

Is he playing the piano?　　No, he isn't.

Is he making a model?　　Yes, he is.

Number 4!

❶ play the piano
❷ play the guitar
❸ play the recorder
❹ make models
❺ make movies
❻ do karate
❼ do gymnastics
❽ play Ping-Pong
❾ play badminton
❿ play volleyball

70 Vocabulary

→ Workbook page 56

5 🎧 6.04 Sing the song.

This is our friend Lizzie.
She's very busy!

She plays badminton on Saturdays,
And she does karate on Sundays.
She makes models after school on Wednesdays,
And she makes movies on Mondays.

She doesn't play on the computer,
And she doesn't watch TV after school.
She plays the guitar in the morning,
And she plays the piano in the afternoon.

We like our friend Lizzie.
She's very busy!

6 Make sentences about the song. Say *true* or *false*.

Lizzie doesn't play badminton on Saturdays.   False!

7 (About Me) Ask and answer with your friend. Then tell another friend.

Do you do karate?

Yes, I do. I do karate on Saturdays.

Sam does karate on Saturdays.

Remember!
She **does** karate on Sundays.
She **doesn't watch** TV after school.
She **plays** the guitar in the morning.

Grammar fun! ▶

8 🎧 6.05 **Look and choose. Then listen and repeat.**

1
Jimmy,
Don't forget tennis club on Tuesday.

Does he play tennis on Tuesdays?
Yes, he does. / No, he doesn't.

2
Leah – Remember volleyball club after school.

Does she play volleyball in the morning?
Yes, she does. / No, she doesn't.

9 🎧 6.06 **Listen and answer the questions.**

10 (About Me) **Ask and answer about your friends.**

Does George do karate after school?

Yes, he does.

11 🎧 6.07 **Go to page 102. Listen and repeat the chant.**

Remember!

Does she do gymnastics in the evening?
Yes, she **does**.   No, she **doesn't**.

Grammar fun! ▶

Grammar

→ Workbook page 58

Skills: *Reading and speaking*

 What sports do you like?

12 🎧 6.08 **Read and listen. Then match.**

a

Sports we like

Meet Josh. He's ten years old, and he wants to be a soccer player.

Josh goes to a soccer club on Tuesdays and Thursdays after school. He plays soccer on Saturdays and Sundays, too. Josh also plays basketball, and he goes swimming.

Josh has a healthy diet. His favorite dinner is chicken with potatoes or rice and vegetables. He likes fruit, too. His favorite drink is a banana milkshake!

b

13 **Read again and answer the questions.**

1 What club does Josh go to?
2 Does he play soccer on Saturdays?
3 Does he play other sports?
4 Does he eat fruits and vegetables?

14 (About Me) **Ask and answer with a friend.**

Do you go to a club after school?
What sports do you play?
Do you have a healthy diet?
Which fruits and vegetables do you like?

Writing

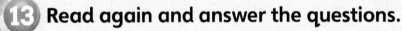

→ Workbook page 59: Write about your favorite sport.

16 **Talk Time** **Listen and repeat. Then act.**

play the guitar   make models   do gymnastics
do karate   play Ping-Pong

Do you want to play Ping-Pong with me?

No, sorry. I can't play Ping-Pong.

Come on – try it!

OK.

Say it!

17 **Listen and repeat.**

Sharks are fish with sharp teeth.

shark

What type of musical instrument is it?

1 🎧 6.12 **Listen and repeat.**

brass   percussion   string   woodwind   piano

2 CLIL ▶ **Watch the video.**

3 **What type of musical instruments can you see?**

Guess What!

A piano is a string instrument and a percussion intrument.

Let's collaborate!

OUR AFTER-SCHOOL BULLETIN BOARD

match   illustrate   design   display   agree   explain

4 **What type of instrument would you like to play?**

→ Workbook page 62   CLIL: Music   **77**

Review

Units 5 and 6

1 Find the words in the puzzles and match to the photographs.

> od scitsanmyg

> yalp llabyellov

> tae a hciwdnas

> netsil ot cisum

2  Listen and say the names.

Kiki

3 Read and say the names.

1 She likes listening to music.
2 He goes to gymnastics club on Tuesdays.
3 She plays volleyball after school.
4 He likes eating sandwiches.

4 Make your own word puzzles for your friend.

> Choose indoor or outdoor activities:
>
> hsaw eht rac
>
> ekam a ekac

James

Evan

Clara

→ Workbook pages 64–65

7 At the market

Look!

Guess What!

3 🎧 7.03 **Listen and say the fruits and vegetables.**

4 Think **Describe and guess what.**

These fruits are small and yellow.   Lemons!

1 lemons
2 limes
3 watermelons
4 coconuts
5 grapes
6 mangoes
7 pineapples
8 pears
9 tomatoes
10 onions

→ Workbook page 66

5 (7.04) Sing the song.

Come and buy some fruit
At my market stall today!

There are lots of pineapples,
And there are some pears,
But there aren't any mangoes
At your market stall today.

Come and buy some fruit
At my market stall today!

There are lots of lemons,
And there are some limes,
But there aren't any tomatoes
At your market stall today.

6 Look at the song and find the differences in this picture.

There are lots of grapes.

7 (About Me) Say what you can buy in your town market.

There are lots of lemons in my town market.

Remember!

There are lots of grapes.
There are some tomatoes.
There aren't any limes.

Grammar fun!

8 🎧 7.05 **Listen and repeat.**

Are there any onions?

Yes, there are.

Are there any coconuts?

No, there aren't.

9 (Think) **Look at the picture. Then cover it and play a memory game.**

mangoes
coconuts
apples
pineapples
watermelons
carrots
onions
beans
limes
lemons
pears
tomatoes

Are there any mangoes?   No, there aren't.

10 (About Me) **Ask and answer about your classroom.**

Are there any books?   Yes, there are.

Remember!
Are there any pears?
Yes, there are.
No, there aren't.

11 🎧 7.06 **Go to page 103. Listen and repeat the chant.**

Grammar fun!

Grammar

→ Workbook page 68

Skills: *Listening and speaking*

Let's start! **Do you like smoothies?**

1

Mango Cooler with ...
Banana
Mango
Orange juice

12 🎧 7.07 **Listen and say the numbers.**

2

Tropical Mix with ...
Pineapple
Banana
Orange juice

Smoothie café

Panini or Roast Bef or BBQ, Coffee:
bagel (Add Bacon!) Swiss or Mayo

3

Tutti Frutti with ...
Pineapple
Grapes
Watermelon

13 🎧 7.08 **Listen again and answer the questions.**

1 Does Emilio like bananas?
2 What are Arianna's favorite fruit?
3 Does Marco like orange juice?

14 (About Me) **Ask and answer with a friend.**

What is your favorite smoothie?
What is your favorite fruit?
Which smoothie don't you like?
Which fruit don't you like?

Writing

➡ Workbook page 69: Write about your favorite smoothie.

Skills **85**

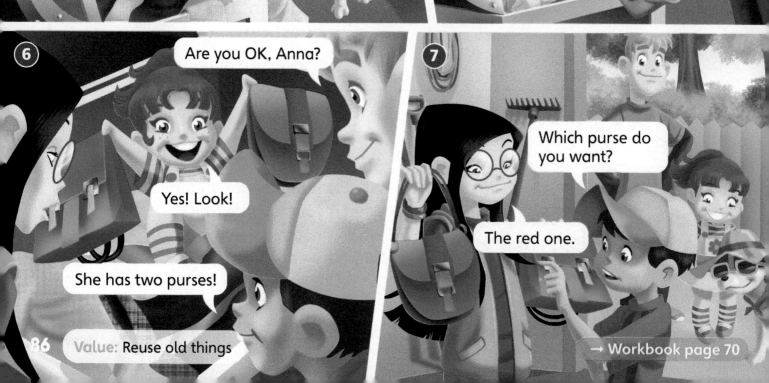

Value: Reuse old things

→ Workbook page 70

16   **Listen and repeat. Then act.**

brown watch   red purse   blue guitar   white radio

Which watch do you want?

The brown one, please.

OK. Here you are.

Say it!

17 🎧 7.11 **Listen and repeat.**

Chipmunks have big cheek pouches.

chipmunk

What parts of plants can we eat?

1 🎧 7.12 **Listen and repeat.**

2 CLIL ▶ **Watch the video.**

3 **Match the fruits and vegetables with the plant parts.**

5 fruit
4 leaf
3 stem
2 root
1 seed

roots
stems
leaves
fruit
seeds

Guess What!
Some plants eat small frogs and lizards.

Let's collaborate!

OUR SALAD STAND

brainstorm
ingredients
discuss
vote
research
create

4 **What plants do you like to eat?**

8 At the beach

Look! ▶

Guess What!

1 🎧 8.01 **Listen and point.**

2 🎧 8.02 **Listen, point, and repeat.**

3 🎧 8.03 **Listen and say the words.**

4 *Think* **Make sentences and guess what.**

Lucas is wearing these. They're black.   Sunglasses!

1 sun
2 burger
3 fries
4 sunglasses
5 swimsuit
6 shorts
7 towel
8 shell
9 ocean
10 sand

5 🎧 8.04 Sing the song.

Which hat is yours?
The red one's mine.
Which hat is yours?
The blue one.

Which sock is hers?
The green one's hers.
Which sock is his?
The yellow one.

Which towel is ours?
The pink one's ours.
Which towel is theirs?
The purple one.

6 Look at the song. Then read and match.

1 Which towel is ours?

2 Which sock is hers?

3 Which hat is yours?

4 Which sock is his?

5 Which towel is theirs?

a The green one's hers. **b** The yellow one's his. **c** The blue one's mine.

d The purple one. **e** The pink one.

7 (About Me) Ask and answer about your classroom.

Which pencil case is yours?

The purple one's mine.

Remember!

Which sock is **hers**?
The green **one's hers**.
Which towel is **theirs**?
The purple **one**.

Grammar fun!

8 🎧 8.05 Listen and repeat.

Whose jacket is this?

It's mine.

Whose shoes are these?

They're Sally's.

9 (About Me) Find these things in your classroom. Then ask and answer.

Whose backpack is this?

It's Mark's.

10 🎧 8.06 Go to page 103. Listen and repeat the chant.

Remember!

Whose glasses are these?
They're mine.

Grammar

→ Workbook page 76

Skills: *Reading and speaking*

 Let's start! **What do you like doing on vacation?**

11 🎧 8.07 **Read and listen. Then match.**

a

Dear Grandma and Grandpa,

We're having a great vacation. Can you see the hotel next to the beach? That's ours!

The beach is great. We like playing in the sand. There are lots of shells. We like making pictures with them.

In the evening, we go to the café on the beach. You can see it in this photograph. I like eating burger and fries. They're delicious!

See you soon!

Love from Louis

b

12 **Read and say *true* or *false*.**

1. Their hotel is next to a forest.
2. They like playing on the beach.
3. There aren't any shells on the beach.
4. Louis likes eating chicken and fries.

13 (About Me) **Ask and answer with a friend.**

Where do you like going on vacation?
Who do you go on vacation with?
What do you do on vacation?
What do you like eating on vacation?

Writing

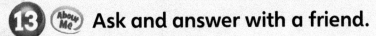 → Workbook page 77: Write a postcard to a friend.

15 🎧 8.09 **Talk Time** **Listen and repeat. Then act.**

| by plane | by bike | on foot | by train | by car | by bus |

1

How should we get to the movie theater?

Let's go by car.

OK. Good idea.

2

How should we get to the beach?

Let's go by bus.

No, let's go by train!

Say it!

16 🎧 8.10 **Listen and repeat.**

Dolphins are friendly and eat fish.

dolphins

→ Workbook page 79   Function: Deciding how to travel   Pronunciation: *ph / f*   **97**

Are sea animals symmetrical?

1 🎧 8.11 Listen and repeat.

① starfish ② crab ③ jellyfish ④ octopus ⑤ sea horse

2 CLIL ▶ Watch the video.

3 In these pictures, which sea animals are symmetrical?

Guess What!

Starfish and octopuses can grow new legs.

①

②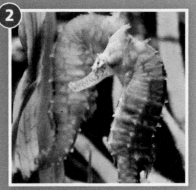

③

④

Let's collaborate!

OUR ECO-VACATION BROCHURE

draft
find out
environment
share tourism
check

4 Which sea animals do you like?

Review

Units 7 and 8

1 Find the words and match to the photographs.

mangoesshellsoceansunglasses

2 🎧 8.12 Listen and say the numbers.

3 Answer the questions.

1 Where are Aiden and his sister playing?

2 Whose shells are on the beach?

3 Are there any mangoes on the beach?

4 Are there any sunglasses at the market?

4 Make your own word puzzles for your friend.

Choose fruits or vegetables:
lemonslimespears

100

→ Workbook pages 82–83

Start

Is there a gym in Lucas's school? (See Unit 2)

Whose painting is this?

Are there any apples at the market? (See Unit 7)

Whose presents are these?

Are there any animals in Lucas's yard? (See Unit 1)

Whose tiger is this?

Whose dog is this?

Are there any shells at the beach? (See Unit 8)

Whose sunglasses are these?

Are there any butterflies in the park? (See Unit 1)

Whose aunt is this?

Is there a computer at Tom's house? (See Unit 5)

Start

#1

101

Chants

Unit 5 (page 62)

 Listen and repeat the chant.

Does he like playing on the computer?
Yes, he does. Yes, he does.
Does she enjoy washing the car?
No, she doesn't. No, she doesn't.

Does she like doing homework?
Yes, she does. Yes, she does.
Does he enjoy reading books?
No, he doesn't. No, he doesn't.

Unit 6 (page 72)

 Listen and repeat the chant.

Does he play tennis on Tuesdays?
Yes, he does. Yes, he does.
Does she play volleyball in the morning?
No, she doesn't. No, she doesn't.

Does he do karate after school?
Yes, he does. Yes, he does.
Does she do gymnastics in the evening?
No, she doesn't. No, she doesn't.

Unit 7 (page 84)

11 **Listen and repeat the chant.**

Are there any onions?
Yes, there are. Yes, there are.
Are there any coconuts?
No, there aren't. No, there aren't.

Are there any pears?
Yes, there are. Yes, there are.
Are there any mangoes?
No, there aren't. No, there aren't.

Unit 8 (page 94)

11 **Listen and repeat the chant.**

Whose jacket is this?
It's mine. It's mine.
Whose shoes are these?
They're Sally's.

Whose backpack is this?
It's Mark's. It's Mark's.
Whose glasses are these?
They're mine.

UPDATED EDITION

Guess What!

Workbook 3 B

with Digital Pack

Contents

American English

Lynne Marie Robertson

Series Editor: Lesley Koustaff

5 Home time

1 Look and match.

a listen to music

b eat a sandwich

c do the dishes

d read a book

e drink juice

f make a cake

g watch TV

h wash the car

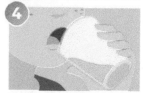

2 Look at activity 1. Complete the sentences.

1 Look at picture 1.   He's _____*reading a book*_____ .

2 Look at picture 2.   He's _____ .

3 Look at picture 4.   She's _____ .

4 Look at picture 6.   She's _____ .

5 Look at picture 7.   He's _____ .

3 (About Me) Answer the questions.

1 Do you like listening to music? _____

2 Do you like playing on the computer? _____

3 Do you like doing homework? _____

My picture dictionary Go to page 84: Find and write the new words.

4 Read and match.

1 I love making cakes.

2 My mom likes listening to music.

3 My sister enjoys doing homework.

4 My brother doesn't enjoy playing this game on the computer.

5 My dad doesn't like doing the dishes.

5 Look and complete the sentences.

| like love doesn't enjoy ~~doesn't like~~ | ~~drink~~ read wash watch |

He _doesn't like drinking_ juice.

She _____ books.

He _____ TV.

She _____ the car.

6 Write about your friend.

Name: _____

1 _____ loves _____ .

2 _____ likes _____ .

3 _____ doesn't enjoy _____ .

7 Look and complete the questions. Then circle the answers.

1 Does he like _____*reading books*_____ ? (Yes, he does.) / No, he doesn't.

2 Does she enjoy _____ ? Yes, she does. / No, she doesn't.

3 Does she like _____ ? Yes, she does. / No, she doesn't.

4 Does he like _____ ? Yes, he does. / No, he doesn't.

5 Does he enjoy _____ ? Yes, he does. / No, he doesn't.

6 Does she like _____ ? Yes, she does. / No, she doesn't.

8 (Think) Look and complete the questions and answers. Then draw.

Does she enjoy ___*making*___ a cake?

No, ___*she doesn't*___ .

_____ enjoy_____ TV?

No, _____ .

_____ love _____ on the computer?

Yes, _____ .

_____ like _____ homework?

Yes, _____ .

Skills: *Writing*

9 **Read the paragraph and write the words.**

love eating   enjoy cleaning   don't like doing   enjoy washing   ~~like making~~

I'm helpful at home. In the morning, I ¹ ___like making___ cakes, and
I ² _____ them! I ³ _____ my bedroom, too. In the
afternoon, I'm helpful. I ⁴ _____ the dog or the car.
After dinner, I'm not helpful. I ⁵ _____ the dishes!

10 (About Me) **Answer the questions.**

1 What do you enjoy cleaning?

I enjoy _____

2 What do you like washing?

_____

3 What do you like making?

_____

4 What do you love doing?

_____

5 What don't you like doing?

_____

11 (About Me) **Write about being helpful at home.**

I'm helpful at home. I like _____

_____

_____

_____

12 (About Me) **Ask and answer with a friend.**

Do you like cleaning your bedroom?   Yes, I do.

13 Read and write the words.

> need   Watch out   so sorry   ~~likes making~~

a

My Aunt Pat *likes making* cakes.

Find a chocolate cake.

Great! Let's go to her house!

b

What do we _____?

Eggs, milk, chocolate …

c

_____, Lucas!

Oh, no!

d

Oh, dear! I'm _____.

Me, too!

14 Look at activity 13. Answer the questions.

1 Where are the children going?   *Aunt Pat's house.*

2 Does Aunt Pat like making cakes?   _____

3 What do they need to make the cake?   _____

4 What does Lucas drop?   _____

5 Who's sorry?   _____

15 Look and check the picture that shows the value: show forgiveness.

16 Color the words that sound like *teeth*. Then answer the question.

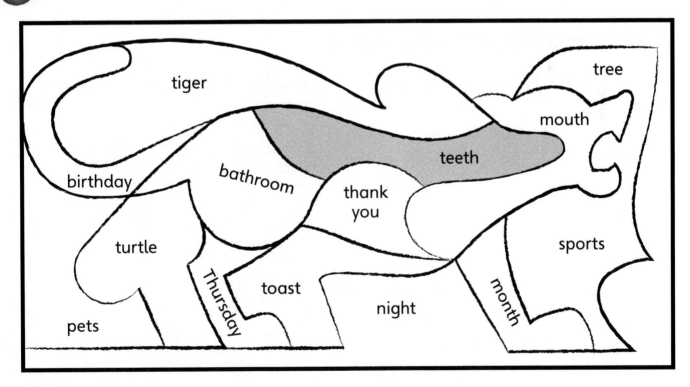

What's this animal? _____

Where do people live?

1 **Find the words and write under the pictures.**

~~wont~~   llivgea   ytic   ouidecyrtns

town

2 **Look and complete the sentences.**

café   houses   riding   stores   supermarket   town   ~~village~~   walking

In the ¹_____village_____ there
is a small ²_____ . There
are two ³_____ . People
like ⁴_____ their bikes there.

In the ⁵_____ , there are a lot
of ⁶_____ and some stores.
You can buy food at the
⁷_____ . A lot of people
are ⁸_____ in the street.

Evaluation

1 **Read and match. Then answer the questions.**

Tom

1	read a book
2	do the dishes
3	do homework
4	listen to music
5	make a cake
6	drink juice

Cara

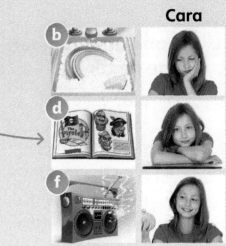

1 Does she like reading a book?   *Yes, she does.*

2 Does she love doing the dishes?   _____

3 Does he like doing homework?   _____

4 Does he enjoy drinking juice?   _____

2 **Look at activity 1. Complete the sentences.**

1 Tom enjoys *doing homework* .

2 Tom loves _____ , but he doesn't like _____ .

3 Cara loves _____ .

4 Cara doesn't enjoy _____ , but she likes _____ .

3 **(About Me) Complete the sentences about this unit.**

1 I can talk about _____ .

2 I can write about _____ .

3 My favorite part is _____ .

4 **(Puzzle) Guess what it is.**

Go to page 88 and circle the answer.

55

6 Hobbies

1 Look and number the picture.

1 play volleyball
2 make movies
3 do gymnastics
4 play the guitar
5 play Ping-Pong
6 play the recorder

2 Look and write the words.

| make   do   ~~play~~   play | models   ~~badminton~~   the piano   karate |

1. _play_
   badminton
2. _____
3. _____
4. _____

3 Write the words from activities 1 and 2 on the lists.

Crafts	Music	Sports
make movies		

My picture dictionary → Go to page 85: Find and write the new words.

4 Look and follow. Then write *true* or *false*.

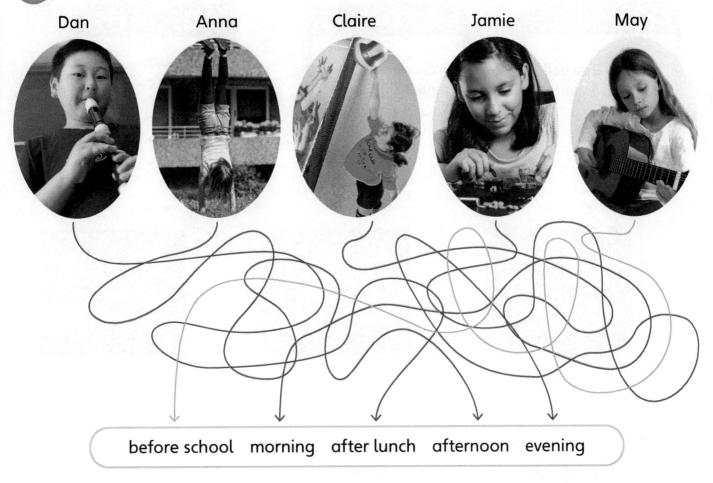

Dan   Anna   Claire   Jamie   May

| before school | morning | after lunch | afternoon | evening |

1 Dan plays the recorder before school. *false*

2 Anna does gymnastics in the afternoon. _____

3 Claire plays volleyball in the evening. _____

4 Jamie makes models in the morning. _____

5 May plays the guitar before school. _____

5 Look at activity 4. Complete the sentences.

1 Dan *doesn't play the recorder* before school.

2 Anna _____ in the afternoon.

3 Claire _____ in the evening.

4 Jamie _____ in the morning.

5 May _____ before school.

6 Look and read. Then answer the questions.

Hi, Jack. Baseball game on Saturday morning.

Jack, remember model club is Tuesday afternoon. Ben

Hello, Jack. Don't forget gymnastics club Tuesday morning before school. Mom

Ella, see you Thursday evening for your piano lesson.

Hi, Ella. Don't forget movie club is Friday evening! Amy

Ella. Remember karate club Sunday morning. Dad

1   Does Jack play baseball on Saturdays?   _Yes, he does._
2   Does Ella play piano in the afternoon?   _____
3   Does Jack make models in the evening?   _____
4   Does Ella make movies on Sundays?   _____
5   Does Jack do gymnastics before school?   _____
6   Does Ella do karate on Sundays?   _____

7 Write questions about Jack and Ella.

> do gymnastics   make movies   make models
> ~~play the guitar~~   play the piano   play volleyball

1   ___Does___ Jack ___play the guitar___ on Saturdays? No, he doesn't.
2   _____ Ella _____ on Thursdays? Yes, she does.
3   _____ Jack _____ on Tuesdays? Yes, he does.
4   _____ Ella _____ in the evening? Yes, she does.
5   _____ Jack _____ in the morning? Yes, he does.
6   _____ Ella _____ on Sundays? No, she doesn't.

Skills: *Writing*

8 **Read the paragraph and write the words.**

after school   competitions   drink   hungry   ~~swimming~~   afternoon

My favorite sport is ¹___swimming___ . I swim every Saturday and Sunday
²_____ . Sometimes there are ³_____ . I'm always
⁴_____ after swimming! I eat a sandwich and ⁵_____
a glass of milk. I enjoy playing tennis, too. We play ⁶_____ on Friday.

9 (About Me) **Answer the questions.**

1 What is your favorite sport?

_My favorite sport is_____

2 When do you do it?

_____

3 Are there any competitions?

_____

4 What do you eat and drink after playing sports?

_____

10 (About Me) **Write about your favorite sport.**

_My favorite sport_____

_____

_____

_____

_____

_____

_____

11 (About Me) **Ask and answer with a friend.**

What's your favorite sport?   My favorite sport is horseback riding.

12 Read and number in order.

Good job, Lucas!

This is fun!

Hi, Lily. Come and play the guitar with me!

OK, great!

Where can we get a guitar?

Let's ask my cousin, Kim. She plays in a band.

1

Here, Lucas. Do you want to play the guitar, too?

No, I'm sorry. I can't play!

Come on, Lucas! Try it.

Practice every day, Lucas.

You can do it, Lucas! Like this …

Oh, dear!

13 Look at activity 12. Circle the answers.

1 Who plays in a band?
   a Tom's cousin   **b Lily's cousin**   c Lily

2 Who wants to play guitar with Kim?
   a Lily   b Anna   c Tom

3 What can't Lucas do?
   a play in a band   b find a guitar   c play the guitar

4 What is fun for Lucas?
   a watching Kim   b trying new things   c playing in a band

5 What does Kim want Lucas to do every day?
   a practice the guitar   b play in Kim's band   c try new things

14 Look and check the pictures that show the value: try new things.

15 Circle the words that sound like *shark*.

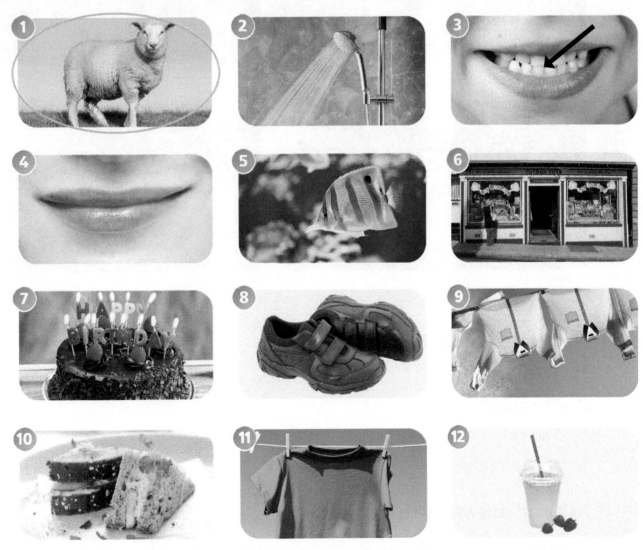

What type of musical instrument is it?

1 Look and guess. Then find and write the words.

girstn   srabs   sserciupon   ~~wwddinoo~~

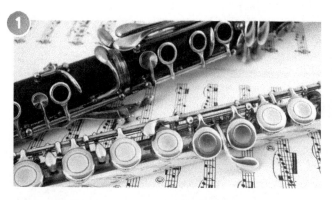

1

woodwind

2

3

4

2 Complete the sentences.

1 The drum _____ is a percussion instrument _____ .

2 The guitar _____ .

3 The piano _____ .

4 The recorder _____ .

3 Ask and answer with a friend.

What instrument do you like?   I like the piano!

Evaluation

1 **Look and complete the Venn diagram. Then answer the questions.**

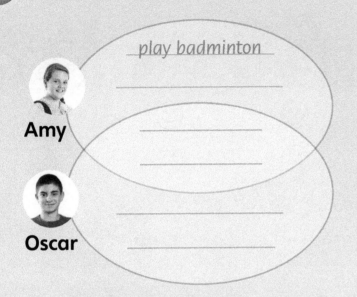

Amy

play badminton

_____

_____

_____

Oscar

_____

Day	Amy	Oscar
Monday morning		
Tuesday after school		
Thursday afternoon		
Friday evening		

1 Does Amy play the piano on Tuesdays? _Yes, she does._

3 Does Amy do karate on Fridays?

_____

2 Does Oscar play the piano on Tuesdays? _____

4 Does Oscar do karate on Tuesdays? _____

2 **Look at activity 1. Complete the sentences about Oscar.**

1 ___He doesn't play___ Ping-Pong after school.

3 _____ karate in the morning.

2 _____ gymnastics on Wednesdays.

4 _____ the piano on Fridays.

3 (About Me) **Complete the sentences about this unit.**

1 I can talk about _____ .

2 I can write about _____ .

3 My favorite part is _____ .

4 (Puzzle) **Guess what it is.**

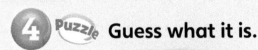
Go to page 88 and circle the answer.

Review Units 5 and 6

1 **Look and answer the questions.**

Jade	☹	☺	☺	☺
Ben	☺	☹	☹	☺

1 Does Ben enjoy playing Ping-Pong? _Yes, he does._

2 Does Jade like playing Ping-Pong? _____

3 Does Ben like reading? _____

4 Does Jade love listening to music? _____

5 Does Ben enjoy playing the guitar? _____

6 Does Jade love playing the guitar? _____

Ben   Jade

2 **Look at activity 1. Complete the sentences.**

1 Jade loves _listening to music_ , but she doesn't like _____ .

2 Ben enjoys _____ , but he doesn't like _____ .

3 Jade likes _____ , but she loves _____ .

4 Ben loves _____ , but he doesn't like _____ .

3 (About Me) **Answer the questions.**

1 Do you like playing Ping-Pong?

_____

2 Do you like playing the guitar?

_____

3 Do you like making lunch?

_____

4 Do you like washing clothes?

_____

4 (Think) **Look and write the verbs on the lists.**

do

1   _do your homework_
2   _____
3   _____

make

4   _____
5   _____
6   _____

play

7   _____
8   _____
9   _____

5 (About Me) **Look at activity 4. Write sentences.**

1   I _____ in the afternoon.
2   I _____ on Saturdays.
3   I like _____ , but _____ .
4   I enjoy _____ , but _____ .

7 At the market

1 Look and do the word puzzle.

Across →

1.
2.
3.
4.
5.
6.

Down ↓

7.
8.
9.

Crossword grid:
1. l e m o n s

2 Think Circle the word that is different. Write a sentence about it.

1 lemons limes (onions) oranges   _Onions are vegetables._
2 mangoes snails limes grapes   _____
3 carrots peas pineapples   _____
4 bananas pears sandwiches   _____

3 About Me Answer the questions.

1 What's your favorite fruit?

My favorite _____

2 What color are they?

_____

3 Are they big or small?

_____

My picture dictionary Go to page 86: Find and write the new words.

Read and circle the correct pictures.

1 There are lots of pineapples.

a    b    c

2 There are some onions.

a    b    c

3 There aren't any tomatoes.

a    b    c

4 There are lots of mangoes.

a    b    c

5 **Look and complete the sentences with *lots of*, *some*, or *not any*.**

1 There _____*aren't any*_____ onions.

2 There _____ vegetables.

3 There _____ bananas.

4 There _____ tomatoes.

5 There _____ carrots.

6 Look and check *yes* or *no*.

		Yes, there are.	No, there aren't.
1	Are there any apples?	☐	✓
2	Are there any carrots?	☐	☐
3	Are there any mangoes?	☐	☐
4	Are there any beans?	☐	☐
5	Are there any watermelons?	☐	☐

7 Look at activity 6. Complete the questions and answers.

1 _____Are there any_____ grapes? _____Yes, there are._____

2 _____ coconuts? _____

3 _____ lemons? _____

4 _____ pineapples? _____

5 _____ oranges? _____

Skills: *Writing*

8 **Read the paragraph and write the words.**

> any   aren't   ~~favorite~~   juice   like   some

My ¹____favorite____ smoothie is Tropical Yum. I like orange ²_____.
It's in my favorite smoothie. Bananas are my favorite fruit. There are
³_____ bananas in my smoothie. There aren't ⁴_____ limes.
I don't ⁵_____ them. They ⁶_____ sweet.

9 **(About Me)** **Answer the questions.**

1   What's your favorite smoothie? Can you think of a name for it?
My favorite smoothie is _____

2   Which juice do you like? Is it in your smoothie?
_____

3   Make a list of the fruit in your smoothie.
_____

4   What fruit don't you like in your smoothie?
_____

10 **(About Me)** **Write about your favorite smoothie.**

My favorite smoothie _____
_____
_____
_____
_____
_____

11 **(About Me)** **Ask and answer with a friend.**

> What's your favorite smoothie?   My favorite smoothie is …

12 **Read and write the words.**

are   has   ~~lots of~~   red   one   don't have

a There are _lots of_ purses.

We _____ any money.

b There _____ lots of old clothes in here.

Great! Let's look for a purse!

c Yes! Look!

She _____ two purses!

d Which purse do you want?

The _____ .

13 **Look at activity 12. Circle the answers.**

1   They're looking for a _____ .
   a (purse)   **b** guitar   **c** hat

2   They don't have any _____ .
   a shoes   **b** old clothes   **c** money

3   There are lots of _____ .
   a new clothes   **b** big clothes   **c** old clothes

4   Anna has _____ .
   a an old purse   **b** two purses   **c** two red purses

5   Lily wants the _____ .
   a blue purse   **b** red purse   **c** new purse

14 Look and check the pictures that show the value: reuse old things.

15 Draw the shapes around the words with the same sound.

□ = sh ◯ = ch

Value   Pronunciation: *ch*   **71**

What parts of plants can we eat?

1 Look and guess. Then find and write the words.

> ~~pragse~~ nabasan sepa insono torcars

grapes

2 Look at activity 1. Read and complete the sentences.

1 They're seeds. They're small. They're green. They're ____peas____ .

2 They're roots. They're orange. Rabbits like eating them. They're _____ .

3 They're purple fruit. We can't buy one. We buy lots of them. They're _____ .

4 They're stems. They're long. We don't eat them for breakfast. They're _____ .

5 They're yellow fruit. Monkeys enjoy eating them. They're _____ .

Evaluation

 1 **Color the fruits and vegetables. Then answer the questions.**

1 Are there any apples? _____ Yes, there are. _____

2 Are there any grapes? _____

3 Are there any pears? _____

4 Are there any watermelons? _____

5 Are there any carrots? _____

6 Are there any pineapples? _____

2 **Write about your classroom.**

> pencils   desks   flowers   ~~books~~   rabbits   windows

1 There are lots of ___ books ___ .   **2** There are some _____ .

3 There aren't any _____ .   **4** _____

5 _____ .   **6** _____

3 **Complete the sentences about this unit.**

1 I can talk about _____ .

2 I can write about _____ .

3 My favorite part is _____ .

4 **Guess what it is.**

Go to page 88 and circle the answer.

1 **Look and write the words. Then color the picture.**

1. Color the _____sun_____ yellow.

2. Next to the towel is a _____ . Color it pink.

3. On the towel are some red and white _____ .

4. Can you see some _____ ? Color them blue.

friesswimsuitoceantowelsandburger

fries

_____

_____

_____

_____

_____

_____

My picture dictionary Go to page 87: Find and write the new words.

3 Think **Look and write the words.**

hers   his   mine   ours   ~~theirs~~   yours

1   Which umbrella is ___theirs___ ? The red one.

2   Which umbrella is _____ ? The purple one.

3   Which sock is _____ ? The white one.

4   Which sock is _____ ? The yellow one.

5   Which hat is _____ ?

6   The green one's _____ .

4 **Look and answer the questions.**

1   Which shell is his?   _The yellow one's his._

2   Which shell is hers?   _____

3   Which towel is theirs?   _____

4   Which towel is ours?   _____

5   Which rabbit is mine?   _____

5 Look and circle the words.

Whose jacket is **that** / **this**?
It's / **They're** Ana's.

Whose shoes are **these** / **those**?
It's / **They're** theirs.

Whose bags are **these** / **those**?
It's / **They're** yours.

Whose sunglasses are **these** / **those**?
It's / **They're** mine.

Whose house is **this** / **that**?
It's / **They're** ours.

6 Look and complete the questions and answers.

Whose hat _is this_ ?

_It's_ his.

_____ bike _____ ?

_____ Tim's.

_____ paintings _____ ?

_____ mine.

_____ pencils _____ ?

_____ theirs.

Skills: *Writing*

7 **Read the postcard and answer the questions.**

1 Where is Dylan? _At the beach._
2 What does he like doing in the morning?
_____
3 Who does he enjoy playing with?
_____
4 What does he do in the afternoon?
_____
5 What does he eat for lunch?
_____

> Dear Renata,
>   We are having a lovely vacation. We're at the beach.
>   I like flying my kite in the morning. I enjoy playing with my sister. In the afternoon, I swim in the ocean. It's great. There are lots of people swimming in the ocean. But there aren't any sharks. ☺
>   At lunchtime we go to the café. I eat sausages and fries.
>   See you soon,
>   Dylan

8 (About Me) **Imagine you're on vacation. Answer the questions.**

1 Where are you?   _I'm_ _____
2 Who is on holiday with you?
_____
3 What do you do in the morning?
_____
4 What do you do in the afternoon?
_____
5 What do you eat?
_____

9 (About Me) **Write a postcard to a friend.**

Dear _____
I'm having a _____
_____
_____
_____

10 (About Me) **Ask and answer with a friend.**

What do you do on vacation?   I swim in the ocean.

11 Read and match.

1 Hi. Do you have my seven things?   2 Good idea. Let's ask my dad.
3 We hope you enjoy it!   4 Thank you, Mr. Lin.

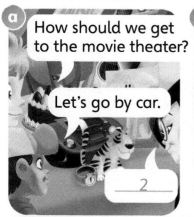

a How should we get to the movie theater?

Let's go by car.

2

Wait a minute! Whose car is that?

It's Aunt Pat's.

Aunt Pat!

d Welcome to our show!

12 Look at activity 11. Circle the answers.

1 Where do they go?
   a to the supermarket   **b** to the school   **c** to the movie theater

2 How do they get there?
   a by bike   **b** by car   **c** by bus

3 How many things do they have?
   a three   **b** five   **c** seven

4 Whose things are they?
   a Lily's   **b** Aunt Pat's   **c** Mr. Lin's

5 What are the things for?
   a family and friends   **b** Anna   **c** a show

13 Look and write the answers. Then check the picture that shows the value: appreciate your family and friends.

Thank you!   ~~Dinner is ready!~~   Five minutes, Mom!   You're a great dad!

1 Dinner is ready!

2

14 Circle the words that sound like *dolphin*.

Are sea animals symmetrical?

1 Look and write the words.

jellyfish   octopus   crab   ~~shell~~   sea horse   starfish

shell

2 Look at activity 1. Write about the sea animals.

1   This shell is small. In this picture, the shell is symmetrical.

2

3

4

5

6

Evaluation

1 Look and do the word puzzle.

Down

Crossword grid:

1 (Across) S _ _ _ _ _ _
6 (Down) S A N D
3 (Across) _ _ _ _
2 (Across)
4 (Across)
5 (Across)
7 (Down)
8 (Down)

2 Look and circle the answers.

1 Whose backpack is this? It's **hers** / (**his**).

3 Which hat is his?
It's the white one. /
It's the red one.

2 Whose ball is this?
It's **his** / **hers**.

4 Which jacket is hers?
It's the green one. /
It's the blue one.

3 (About Me) Complete the sentences about this unit.

1 I can talk about _____ .

2 I can write about _____ .

3 My favorite part is _____ .

4 (Puzzle) Guess what it is.

Go to page 88 and circle the answer.

Review Units 7 and 8

1 Look and answer the questions.

1	Are there any shorts?	_Yes, there are._
2	Are there any sunglasses?	_____
3	Are there any shells?	_____
4	Is there a swimsuit?	_____
5	Is there a towel?	_____
6	Are there any pineapples?	_____
7	Are there any lemons?	_____
8	Is there a watermelon?	_____
9	Are there any onions?	_____
10	Are there any coconuts?	_____

2 Look and match. Complete the sentences with *some*, *lots of*, or *not any*.

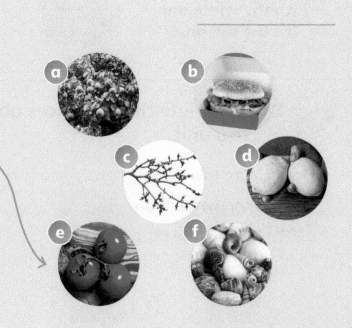

1	_There are some_	tomatoes.
2	_____	pears.
3	_____	lemons.
4	_____	shells.
5	_____	grapes.
6	_____	fries.

3 Look and circle the words.

1 Whose pineapple is (this) / that?

(It's) / They're yours.

2 Whose onions are these / those?

It's / They're yours.

3 Whose limes are these / those?

It's / They're mine.

4 Whose shell is this / that?

It's / They're mine.

4 Think Look and circle the words. Then answer the questions.

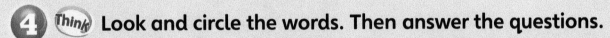

1 Which camera is **hers** / (**yours**)?

The small one's mine.

2 Which kite is **his** / **yours**?

_____

3 Which pencil case is **his** / **ours**?

_____

4 Which towel is **his** / **theirs**?

_____

5 Which bag is **hers** / **his**?

_____

(5) Home time

do homework   watch TV   ~~do the dishes~~   listen to music   wash the car
play on the computer   drink juice   make a cake   read a book   eat a sandwich

do the dishes

6 Hobbies

play the recorder   play Ping-Pong   do karate   play badminton   make models
play the guitar   make movies   play the piano   ~~do gymnastics~~   play volleyball

do gymnastics

onions ~~coconuts~~ watermelons mangoes pineapples
tomatoes limes pears lemons grapes

coconuts

_____

_____

_____

_____

_____

_____

_____

_____

_____

swimsuit   fries   shells   sun   ~~burger~~   sunglasses   sand   towel   ocean   shorts

burger

My puzzle

1 Find the words ↓ →. Use the colored letters to answer the question.

P	G	P	I	B	R	A	R	Y	A	R	A	U	B
I	Q	L	R	T	G	Y	J	K	E	L	P	V	E
N	P	A	B	U	T	T	E	R	F	L	Y	U	V
E	B	Y	M	S	W	L	H	B	G	T	D	A	M
A	M	T	F	O	T	D	W	B	I	I	S	O	A
P	G	H	A	O	S	H	O	W	E	R	H	X	T
P	A	E	N	M	G	I	R	C	M	Q	E	Z	H
L	S	G	N	H	K	L	U	Y	O	O	L	P	M
E	M	U	A	E	T	R	E	R	E	S	L	L	Y
X	V	I	E	B	G	H	Y	O	P	W	F	R	Y
D	O	T	H	E	D	I	S	H	E	S	O	K	R
J	K	A	S	K	V	B	Y	U	W	E	T	R	E
M	L	R	W	T	E	C	J	F	G	A	N	N	A

Q: What are two fruits people can buy at the market?

A: ___ ___ ___ ___ ___ ___   and   ___ ___ ___ ___ ___

Acknowledgments

Many thanks to everyone in the excellent team at Cambridge University Press & Assessment in Spain, the UK, and India.

The authors and publishers would like to thank the following contributors:

Blooberry Design: concept design, cover design, book design
Hyphen: publishing management, page make-up
Ann Thomson: art direction
Gareth Boden: commissioned photography
Jon Barlow: commissioned photography
Ian Harker: class audio recording
John Marshall Media: "Grammar fun" recordings
Robert Lee, Dib Dib Dub Studios: song and chant composition
Vince Cross: theme tune composition
James Richardson: arrangement of theme tune
Phaebus: "CLIL" video production
Kiki Foster: "Look!" video production
Bill Smith Group: "Grammar fun" and story animations
Sounds Like Mike Ltd: "Grammar Fun" video production

The authors and publishers acknowledge the following sources of copyright material and are grateful for the permissions granted. While every effort has been made, it has not always been possible to identify the sources of all the material used, or to trace all copyright holders. If any omissions are brought to our notice, we will be happy to include the appropriate acknowledgements on reprinting and in the next update to the digital edition, as applicable.

Key: U = Unit.

Student's Book

Photography

The following photos are sourced from Getty Images:
U5: Marc Debnam/Photodisc; Ryan McVay/Photodisc; Pablo Alberto Velasco Ibarra/EyeEM; slowmotiongli/iStock/Getty Images Plus; lucky-photographer/iStock Editorial; Mimadeo/iStock/Getty Images Plus; Subodh Agnihotri/iStock/Getty Images Plus; Goads Agency/E+; Lane Oatey/Blue Jean Images/blue jean images; Dev Carr/Image Source; Kraig Scarbinsky/DigitalVision; Wealan Pollard/OJO Images; Hill Street Studios/DigitalVision; U6: TadejZupancic/E+; monkeybusinessimages/iStock/Getty Images Plus; Jose Luis Pelaez Inc/DigitalVision; Erik Isakson/Tetra images; Barry Downard; Hugh Sitton/Stone; Gary S Chapman/Photographer's Choice; Mr_Twister/iStock/Getty Images Plus; Salvator Barki/Moment; Nick Rowe/Stockbyte; Scott Van Dyke/Corbis Documentary;SEAN GLADWELL/Moment; PhotoAlto Agency Collections; Dhemmy Zeirifandi; mbbirdy/E+; mladn61/E+; Wattanaphob Kappago; Westend61; Terry Vine/DigitalVision; PhotoAlto/PhotoAlto Agency Collections; U7: rudi_suardi/iStock Unreleased; Kingfisher Productions/DigitalVision; George Contorakes; szefei/iStock/Getty Images Plus; Phillip Hayson/Stockbyte; mbbirdy/E+; Richard Clark/The Image Bank; dogayusufdokdok/E+; Creativeye99/E+; MW/Stockbyte; ruizluquepaz/E+; Mike Kemp/Tetra images; U8: A bflo photo/Moment Open; Barry Downard; Stuart Westmorland/Corbis Documentary; Medioimages/Photodisc; SolStock/E+; Jose Luis Pelaez Inc/DigitalVision; Elisabeth Schmitt/Moment; JulPo/E+; Floortje/E+; FatCamera/E+; RedHelga/iStock/Getty Images Plus.

The following photos are sourced from other libraries:
U5: Adrian Cook/Alamy; D. Hurst/Alamy; Jim West/Alamy; LanKS/Shutterstock; James Osmond/Alamy; Christopher Hill/scenicireland.com/Alamy; Russ Munn/Design Pics Inc/Alamy; incamerastock/Alamy; Scenics & Science/Alamy; Ingvar Bjork/Alamy; U6: Inti St Clair/Tetra Images, LLC/Alamy; Zhelunovych/Shutterstock; AiVectors/Shutterstock; nattanan726/Shutterstock; Denis Scott/Corbis; exopixel/Shutterstock; the palms/Shutterstock; Kitch Bain/Shutterstock; Discovod/Shutterstock; Ansis Klucis/Shutterstock; Smileus/Shutterstock; Denys Kurylow/Shutterstock; Tom Pavlasek/Shutterstock; Sergio Schnitzler/Shutterstock; Tetra Images/Alamy; muzsy/Shutterstock; Radius Images/Design Pics/Alamy; U7: Valeri Luzina/Shutterstock; Linda Freshwaters Arndt/Alamy; MIXA/SOURCENEXT/Alamy; B. BOISSONNET/BSIP SA/Alamy; Filipe B. Varela/Shutterstock; Sergii Figurnyi/Shutterstock; JIANG HONGYAN/Shutterstock; Yasonya/Shutterstock; Richard Griffin/Shutterstock; vnlit/Shutterstock; Africa Studio/Shutterstock; Crepesoles/Shutterstock; photosync/Shutterstock; Dulce Rubia/Shutterstock; Preto Perola/Shutterstock; U8: LOOK Die Bildagentur der Fotografen GmbH/Alamy; Juergen Richter/Image Professionals GmbH/Alamy; silvae/Shutterstock; WaterFrame_fba/Alamy; David Fleetham/Alamy; aquapix/Shutterstock; sunsinger/Shutterstock; L. Powell/Shutterstock; melissaf84/Shutterstock; Keith Tarrier/Shutterstock; Damsea/Shutterstock; Sergii Figurnyi/Shutterstock; Henry Beeker/Alamy; Ivonne Wierink/Shutterstock; Terry Mathews/Alamy; Elena Schweitzer/Shutterstock.

Workbook

Photography

The following photos are sourced from Getty Images:
U5: Jose Luis Pelaez Inc/DigitalVision; Michael Marquand/Getty; luckyphotographer/iStock Editorial/Getty Images Plus; U6: TadejZupancic/E+; George Doyle/Stockbyte; Marilyn Nieves/E+; Hugh Sitton/Stone; yenwen/E+; Scott Van Dyke/Corbis Documentary; Rubberball/Erik Isakson; U7: Gonzalo Azumendi/Getty; rudi_suardi/iStock Unreleased; U8: A bflo photo/Moment Open; Stuart Westmorland/Corbis Documentary; Dan Fairchild Photography/Moment Open; Photodisc.

The following photos are sourced from other libraries:
U5: Adrian Cook/Alamy; p_ponomareva/Shutterstock; Ground Picture/Shutterstock; MBI/Alamy; Deborah Vernon/Alamy; LanKS/Shutterstock; antb/ Shutterstock; Videowokart/Shutterstock; Boris Stroujko/Shutterstock; dbtravel/Alamy; Joe Cox/Shutterstock; Sergey Novikov/Shutterstock; goodluz/Shutterstock; U6: p_ponomareva/Shutterstock; Mikhail Kondrashov "fotomik"/Alamy; Monkey Business Images/Shutterstock; DAJ/amana images inc./Alamy; Jana Fernow/Westend61 GmbH/Alamy; Sonderegger Christof/Prisma by Dukas Presseagentur GmbH/Alamy; wentus/Shutterstock; Vector Shutterstock/Shutterstock; Bipsun/Shutterstock; nattanan726/Shutterstock; Tom Bird/Shutterstock; lendy16/Shutterstock; mikute/Shutterstock; ntstudio/Shutterstock; Anna Lurye/Shutterstock; T.M.O.Buildings/Alamy; Romiana Lee/Shutterstock; Rob Hyrons/Shutterstock; Radka Tesarova/Shutterstock; Wiktory/Shutterstock; Mike Flippo/Shutterstock; M. Unal Ozmen/Shutterstock; Richard T. Nowitz/Corbis; redsnapper/Alamy; Bob Daemmrich/Alamy; Maxim Tarasyugin/Shutterstock; cristovao/Shutterstock; eurobanks/Shutterstock; Tatiana Popova/Shutterstock; Mendelex/Shutterstock; Attl Tibor/Shutterstock; bogdan ionescu/Shutterstock; EKS design/Shutterstock; Edith Held/Corbis; U7: Candace Hartley/Shutterstock; Daniel M Ernst/Shutterstock; George Dolgikh/Shutterstock; sjk2012/Shutterstock; Mukesh Kumar/Shutterstock; Antonova Ganna/Shutterstock; IngridHS/Shutterstock; Nataliya Arzamasova/Shutterstock; Paulo Vilela/Shutterstock; Lex0077/Shutterstock; Valeri Luzina/Shutterstock; nodff/Shutterstock; yykkaa/Shutterstock; Matt9122/Shutterstock; CREATISTA/Shutterstock; Africa Studio/Shutterstock; Studio Light and Shade/Shutterstock; MIXA/SOURCENEXT/Alamy; Fabio Bernardi/Shutterstock; bergamont/Shutterstock; Kuttelvaserova Stuchelova/Shutterstock; Lukas Gojda/Shutterstock; Jiri Hera/Shutterstock; Kozub Vasyl/Shutterstock; U8: foodfolio/Alamy; Denis Tabler/Shutterstock; A. Kiro/Shutterstock; Luisa Leal Photography/Shutterstock; Slavica Stajic/Shutterstock; stockcreations/Shutterstock; silvae/Shutterstock; Juergen Faelchle/Shutterstock; Maryna Kulchytska/Shutterstock; Kondrachov Vladimir/Shutterstock; Donovan van Staden/Shutterstock; jannoon028/Shutterstock; Studio 1231/Shutterstock; Andrei Armiagov/Shutterstock; Rocketclips, Inc./Shutterstock; Antlii/Shutterstock; Anna Klepatckaya/Shutterstock; Evocation Images/Shutterstock; QiuJu Song/Shutterstock; Orange Dog Studio/Shutterstock; Vittorio Bruno/Shutterstock; Cuson/Shutterstock; Mirek Kijewski/Shutterstock; Songchai W/Shutterstock; pyzata/Shutterstock; SvedOliver/Shutterstock; Alex from the Rock/Shutterstock; Elena Shashkina/Shutterstock; Cherry-Merry/Shutterstock; Steve Skjold/Alamy; iPiCfootage/Shutterstock; Filip Fuxa/Shutterstock; givaga/Shutterstock; SB Freelancer/Shutterstock; Tei Sinthip/Shutterstock; Thomas Dutour/Shutterstock; Anna Biancoloto/Shutterstock.

Front Cover Photography by Olena Kuzina/iStock/Getty Images Plus.

Illustrations

Aphik; A Corazon Abierto; Luke Newell; Marcus Cutler; Mark Duffin; Pablo Gallego; Brian Lee; Gareth Conway (Bright Agency); Graham Kennedy; Humberto Blanco (Sylvie Poggio); Ilias Arahovitis (Beehive Illustration); Monkey Feet; Simon Walmesley.